OCCASIONAL

THE PEOPLE ON THE EDGE:

Religious Reform and the Burden of the Western Muslim Intellectual

ABDELWAHAB EL-AFFENDI

THE INTERNATIONAL INSTITUTE OF ISLAMIC THOUGHT

LONDON · WASHINGTON

THE INTERNATIONAL INSTITUTE OF ISLAMIC THOUGHT
LONDON OFFICE
P.O. BOX 126, RICHMOND, SURREY TW9 2UD, UK
WWW.IIITUK.COM

USA OFFICE
P.O. BOX 669, HERNDON, VA 20172, USA
WWW.IIIT.ORG

ISBN 978-1-56564-357-4

Typesetting by Sideek Ali
Cover design by Sohail Nakhooda
Printed in the United Kingdom by Cromwell Press Group

SERIES EDITORS

DR. ANAS S. AL SHAIKH-ALI
SHIRAZ KHAN

FOREWORD

THE INTERNATIONAL INSTITUTE OF ISLAMIC THOUGHT (IIIT) London Office has great pleasure in presenting Occasional Paper 19: *The People on the Edge: Religious Reform and the Burden of the Western Muslim Intellectual* by Dr. Abdelwahab El-Affendi.

The IIIT was established in 1981, and has served as a major center to facilitate serious scholarly efforts based on Islamic vision, values and principles. Its programs of research, seminars and conferences for the last twenty-eight years have resulted in the publication of more than two hundred and fifty titles under different series in English and Arabic, many of which have been translated into several other languages.

In 1989 the London Office initiated the Occasional Papers series, a set of easy to read booklets designed to present, in concise format, research papers, articles and lectures from the Institute's worldwide program as well as from scholars and social scientists willing to make contributions. To date fifteen papers have been published in the series the last of which was in 2008, with several being translated into French and German.

We would like to express our thanks and gratitude to Dr. Abdelwahab El-Affendi as well as the editorial and production team and those who were directly or indirectly involved in the completion of this paper. May God reward them and the author for all their efforts.

ANAS S. AL SHAIKH-ALI, CBE
Muharram 1431 AH, *January, 2010*

THE PEOPLE ON THE EDGE: RELIGIOUS REFORM AND THE BURDEN OF THE WESTERN MUSLIM INTELLECTUAL*

THERE is a haunting and very powerful image in the Qur'an, depicting a category of people who, on the Day of Judgement, would be perched on the dividing barrier between heaven and hell, and from that point engage in a conversation with the inhabitants of both worlds (Qur'an, 7: 46-49). The portrayal, which occurs only once in the Qur'an, is vague about the ultimate fate of these "people of the edge," but there are hints, in addition to the generally sympathetic portrayal, that they will end up on the safer side of the barrier.

Apocalyptic images may seem appropriate to depict the dilemmas facing the beleaguered Muslim communities in the West in the bleak post-9/11 era. Even without the rising hostility to Muslim presence in the West, emigrant communities have already been facing the challenge of adapting to exogenous cultural norms and values, making it an uphill task to maintain an "authentic Muslim life."[1] As a consequence of the adjustments needed to accommodate Islam's minority status, it has been argued, "[t]he Islam of Muslim intellectuals in the West tends to assume a more ethereal character." The concrete manifestations of this tendency include the advocacy Sufism because "it is private enough to fit into the Western social order and it is public enough to remain an echo of the total Islamic order."[2] This in turn makes it "a reasonable hypothesis that Islam – or the way Muslim life is led – is likely to change a great deal in cases where religion is more or less forced into the private corner of one's life."[3]

*An earlier version of this paper has been published in the *Harvard Middle Eastern and Islamic Review* 8 (2009), pp.19–50. The author currently holds a fellowship from the Economic and Social Research Council (ESRC) and the Arts & Humanities Research Council (AHRC). He would like to thank both councils for support with his research.

For many Western Muslim intellectuals and some observers, however, this uncertain status of being "on the edge" may in fact be an advantage. Residing securely in the paradise of modernity, prosperity and "enlightenment," these intellectuals are also confident that they do, simultaneously, speak both to, and for, the rest of the Muslim community, seen to have been "left behind" in the purgatory of turmoil and darkness. As one prominent Western Muslim intellectual put it, "standing with one leg in the Orient and with the other one in the Occident" permits one to "understand both worlds sufficiently well to explain them to each other."[4]

With an increasing number of Muslim intellectuals achieving prominence in the West, from where they had seen their ideas and views widely propagated and discussed from the heart of Anatolia to the remote corners of Africa, Western Muslim intellectuals have reason to view their role with increased self-confidence. Especially in the US, where we can observe an unparalleled "high concentration of Muslim elites... particularly in the university system," it has been argued that we are currently witness to "a critical evaluation of religious texts not seen since at least the colonial period."[5] This may have already led to a shift in the intellectual centre of gravity away from traditional Muslim heartlands, with the United States fast becoming a major "world center of Islamic learning and intellectual life and thought," even potentially a "second Mecca."[6] In fact, it is claimed, there is today,

> much more intellectual Islamic life in the West than in the East. More serious books on Islam are being published in English than in Arabic... And since Muslim thinkers in the West can write without censorship, their production is likely to be essential for the development of Islam in the Muslim world. I think the Muslims in America and in Europe will be the leaders for the intellectual revitalization of the Muslims in the East.[7]

The efforts of US-based Muslim intellectuals to critically undermine the bases of authoritarianism in Islamic thought could warrant an "even more ambitious agenda following up on changes in Islam's ideology with changes in leadership and religious practices."[8]

There is much that justifies these ambitions, but one must guard against the imperceptible shift from ambition to illusion. To move from a valid appreciation of the increasing importance of the intellectual contribution of western Muslims to a "wag the dog" theory of ascribing to them a leadership role in religious reform may be as misguided – and as dangerous – an illusion as the idea that creating an American colony in Iraq was going to be an advertisement of America's love for democracy, and an inspiration for freedom lovers all over the Muslim world. Both illusions spring from the same quintessentially Western overconfidence, not to say arrogance, of which Muslim westerners are not immune.

In this paper, we argue that while Muslim intellectual activism in the West had deep historical roots and illustrious antecedents, the claims of the new emerging movements and intellectual figures to moral, intellectual and religious leadership of the Ummah are unprecedented in their boldness and pride in their specifically western/modernist credentials. Moreover, it is paradoxical that what is in essence a response to the precariousness of the increasingly vulnerable Muslim presence in the West is at the same time trying to present itself at the most authoritative interpretation of Islam. The paper traces the historical roots of western Muslim intellectual activism, and outlines the shifts and dynamics which gave its present form and conditioned its attempts to turn its vulnerability into an asset. It shows the ways in which the claims of the major contending trends within western Islam are novel, and assesses their success in attracting support both within the West and the wider Muslim world. We conclude that while the positions staked by these emerging trends are legitimate and significant, their claims for leadership are shaky and premature. They seem to be based on a misconception of the dynamics and sources of religious authority, which cannot be divorced from issues of identity within the religious community. Pride in being Western at a time of perceived conflict between Islam and the West becomes counterproductive unless the intellectuals can make an effective contribution to resolving or at least tempering this conflict. In addition, challenging an established religious tradition requires more than the mere intellectual elaboration of a position, but must mobilize the deep spiritual resources of that tradition in support of the new position. The moral authority of the potential reformist is also closely linked to an ability to articulate Muslim concerns and the courage not only to challenge accepted tradition, but also to stand up to the powers that be.

A PRECARIOUS EXISTENCE

The excessive confidence of the spokespersons of Western Islam contrasts sharply with the doubly precarious Muslim presence in the West, both in terms of the relatively hostile environment and in terms of the pressures of secular political and intellectual hegemony. In an environment where the best Muslim is the "integrated" (read invisible) one, Muslim self-consciousness here is a fairly recent development, and it has crystallized in adverse circumstances of turmoil and conflict that make the preoccupation with survival and adaptation a central feature of this emerging self-consciousness. The circumstances surrounding specifically Muslim activism, and the assertion of *Muslim* identity in Europe and the West, were largely a reaction to adverse developments, either abroad or in the West. Events from the Algerian war of independence in the 1950s to the Algerian civil war in the 1990s (with Suez, Palestine, Kashmir, Bosnia, the Iranian revolution and the Iraq wars in between) have deeply impacted the psyche of Muslims living in the West and conditioned their attitude towards their countries of residence. Algerians (and other Muslims) living in France, for example, organized protests in support of the Algerian resistance, while Arab journalists working in the BBC refused to work, or resigned altogether, during the Suez crisis of 1956. The Israeli invasion of Lebanon in 1982 and the Palestinian *intifada* (from 1987), brought Muslim protestors to the streets in European cities in increasing numbers, often under Islamic banners.

Events within the West also worked to shape the self-awareness of Muslim communities here. These included the Salman Rushdie[9] affair in Britain (1989) the headscarf controversy in France (from 1989) and the Bosnian war of 1991-1995. Such events had the cumulative impact of sharpening the sense of Muslim identity and derivatively increasing the visibility of Muslims *as Muslims*. Direct involvement by the US and major European powers in the wars on Iraq (from 1990) has tested the loyalties of some Muslim citizens in these countries to the limit. While Muslim agitation over issues like Iraq and Bosnia attracted solidarity from non-Muslim protestors (in spite of persistent Muslim complaints of insufficient support), the protests over the Rushdie affair or the headscarf bans were mostly a lonely Muslim affair.

By the time the September 11 atrocities in the United States (2001) were perpetrated, this process of polarization and differentiation of the Muslim community from the rest of society was already well advanced. The Madrid bombings of March 11, 2004 and, last but not least, the London bombings of July 7, 2005, only helped it along. The resulting and progressive polarization of identities set Muslims apart from other immigrants as well as from the rest of their European or American compatriots, and united Muslims from different backgrounds around common causes and a shared identity. Being a Muslim became a much more salient identity than wider identities shared with other communities ('immigrant', 'black', 'Asian', 'citizen', etc.), as well as narrower identities which had formerly been more meaningful for those involved ('Punjabi', 'Palestinian', 'Malay', 'Nigerian', etc.).

The emergence and crystallization of the Muslim presence in the context of these conflicts inevitably cast this "rise of Islam" in a negative light. The Rushdie Affair represented a turning point in this regard, for it brought together issues that elicited serious and deep concerns in the minds of Western intellectuals and policy makers.[10] This was especially the case since liberal and radical intellectuals who habitually supported Muslims as a disadvantaged community against perceived racism or xenophobia found it difficult to back Muslim demands in this instance. Some former 'liberal' or left leaning intellectuals have become very vociferous critics of Islam and

Muslims, often using language that will be difficult to distinguish from that habitually used by ultra-right wing thinkers.[11] It is no coincidence that the headscarf controversy in France had erupted in that period, which also coincided with a sharp rise in support for extreme right wing movements across Europe. The self-awareness of Muslims as Muslims was thus accompanied by a corresponding (often, but not always, negative) awareness of the 'alien' presence and visibility of 'Muslims' as a supposedly homogenous group embracing Arabs and Africans, Asians and Turks. This in turn tended to displace some earlier stereotypes of Asians, immigrants, or blacks, in the direction of one single community, with less guilt and self-consciousness.

The salience of Muslim identity and the sharpening of Muslim self-awareness have thus become integral to a dynamic process of adaptation to perceived adverse trends and threats, and in turn elicited more hostile reactions from wider sections of society at large. For example Muslim representative institutions created in Europe and the US themselves became targets for attacks from the media and rival lobby groups as either unrepresentative or extremist. It is in order to break out of this vicious circle that the new trends of thought and activism had emerged seeking to forge a new Muslim identity that could be more easily reconciled with Western identity.

EURO-ISLAM AND THE SECOND MAKKAH

It may be difficult in these circumstances to see in the beleaguered Muslim communities in the West a beacon of light for the wider Muslim community. But some European Muslims, while acknowledging the current crisis and the deep roots of the identity clash, struggle to point out the positive side of this dilemma. Tracing the mythical roots of the Islam/west identity polarization even further back, one writer seeks inspiration in symbolic depictions from early modern art, specifically in Rembrandt's drawings of Abraham's casting out of Hagar and her son Ishmael. One drawing shows "Hagar, young and fertile, being sent forth into the wilderness at the behest of Sarah, the infant Ishmael by her side. Sarah, the indigene, the Hebrew, is portrayed as an old, infertile woman, who looks at the departing refugee from an upper window."[12]

That myth of expulsion is now being played in the reverse:

> Today, in Europe, Sarah is again old, and Hagar is again fertile. Islam is, as we would theologically expect, at the forefront of the reinvigoration of the tired demography of a continent which, in living memory, has seen terrible nightmares. Ishmael, the refugee, uncontaminated by Europe's crimes, is now settling in Europe. He has, in fact, already become Europe's most significant Other. He thus brings hope that Europe's appalling history may find an alternative path, a vision of God and society that can heal the continent's wounds.[13]

While the conduct of an extremist Muslim fringe has given adequate ammunition for habitual European xenophobia, this writer adds, one should look at the positive side of this encounter. With vociferous demands that they should "integrate," Muslims find themselves "at the centre of Europe's current debate about itself." These demands to integrate appear as problematic as they are pregnant with possibilities. The Muslims can, in redefining themselves, redefine Europe's identity at the same time. "Islam can easily define itself as another trans-national strand in the tapestry of the changing and broadening European reality."[14]

In defining themselves as "an EU-wide community, with a particular moral and spiritual vocation to a largely secularized region of the world," European Muslims can easily resolve the integration dilemma and refute accusations that Islam "forbids integration, and creates a politically and socially dangerous ghetto."

> The evolution of a European Islam, absolutely faithful to the religion's duties but open to the European mainstream, will also help governments, and the European parliament, to distinguish between authentic Islam, and the Islam of extreme sects and factions currently being exported by a few corners of the Islamic world.[15]

According to some protagonists in this drama, this distinctive "European Muslim" identity is already slowly taking shape, helped by the evolution of new institutions and attitudes. A "burgeoning European Islam" can already be observed, taking its place beside African, Central Asian or Malay Islam. And it will, these protagonists believe, resolve in a decisive way the ongoing crises of identity and problems of integration facing European Muslims.

The idea that a specifically European Islam (or Euro-Islam) is in fact desirable, necessary and actually emerging is being propagated by advocates ranging from the current French President Nicola Sarkozy (in his former status as Interior Minister), who called for "a French Islam and not an Islam in France," to secular Muslim intellectuals such as Bassam Tibi (Germany) and Muhammad Arkoun (France), and finally Islamic intellectuals and activists such as Tariq Ramadan and the leaders of various Muslim youth groups in Europe. The idea has also many natural proponents in the increasing number of native European converts (or indigenous European Muslims in the Balkans) who could not help being Muslim and European at the same time. This Euro-Islam is characterized, according to its proponents, by fundamental revisions of traditional Islamic law and norms to adapt to the existence of Muslims in predominantly non-Muslim lands governed by secular, pluralistic and democratic norms. It also exhibits a tendency towards the creation of a new "real European Islamic culture," dominated by new forms of "artistic expression [that] are slowly disengaging from their specifically Arab, Turkish or Indo-Pakistani antecedents, and are attempting to recreate Islamic values within national mores and cultural tastes."[16]

Increasing financial independence from sources of funding in the Middle East and elsewhere in the Muslim world, and progressive institutionalization of Muslim communities in the West, coupled with the integration of these communities and their representative institutions into the wider social and political structures, are among the many signs of the emergence of a vibrant and genuinely European Islam. The integration of Muslims into Europe will thus not be a "passive" act of conforming to existing norms, but a positive one of "building a new Europe" that would be richer and better.[17]

The transition from this modest, if rather controversial, demand for adapting Islam to Europe to the more ambitious claim that the resulting synthesis could be exported back to the wider Muslim world as a superior and more modernity-friendly version of Islam was left to (who else?) North American Muslims. Here, increasingly bold claims are being made not just of evolving a more "progressive" version of Islam, but one that is indispensable to saving Muslims from themselves.[18]

One has to note here that the more "modest" European claim is not that modest to start with. The very concept of "Euro-Islam" is deeply problematic. While the comparison to "African" or "Asian" Islam is pertinent, it must be pointed out that no one had set out consciously to create an "African" or "Asian" Islam. That would have been considered sheer heresy from the perspective of traditional Islamic orthodoxy. As in most other religious traditions, observance is subject to geographical and historical variations. However, none of these came as a result of a conscious strategy to adapt to local exigencies. In fact such variations usually emerge in spite of serious attempts at faithful adherence to an "original" blueprint.

This point is further underlined by the impact of the current "Islamic revival," of which the self-assertion of European Muslims is but one manifestation. Revivalism has in fact been rolling back the idiosyncrasies and regional variations of Islamic observance in favor of a stricter conformity to "orthodoxy" or a more "universal" Islam.[19] While many scholars complain that this pressure to conform comes from insidious Wahhabi influence bankrolled by Saudi oil money,[20] the process is much more complex than that. Modernization in general, it has been argued, has favored the retreat of so called "popular Islam" which embodied these cultural variations in favor of the "high Islam" of the text-oriented orthodox *ʿulamāʾ*.[21] Some of the proponents of "Euro-Islam" thus see in it the antithesis of "fundamentalist" revivalism,[22] even though the more serious contenders in the effort to fashion "Euro-Islam" happen to hail from the revivalist camp.

To have any chance of being a credible alternative, Euro-Islam is conscious of the need to take the religious establishment (and the more moderate revivalist trends) on board, and not only in Europe. For it is an inescapable fact that, in this age of global reach, no "Islam" or any other system of thought for that matter, could enjoy the luxury of isolation of the pre-modern Muslim communities in remote African or Central and East Asian localities. That is why, in spite of celebrating their institutional and intellectual independence, proponents of Euro-Islam feel the need to enlist the help of a number of prominent religious scholars from Muslim heartlands to formulate their new rethinking of Islamic norms.[23] A conference held in London in February 2005 tried precisely to mobilize such support for a new rethinking of Islam "for minorities," inviting a host of *ʿulamāʾ* from key Muslim countries to lead the debate.[24] When Tariq Ramadan issued his call for suspending Islamic punishments (in an article published in *Le Monde* on April 1, 2005), he defended himself by claiming that he had secured the agreement of key traditional *ʿulamāʾ* to his thesis, adding that few of them have been prepared to back him up in public.[25]

Be that as it may, the claims of Euro-Islam centre on a demand for "autonomy" from the wider Ummah and its perceptions and concerns. The focus is adaptation to a specific environment, and on the right to be different from other Muslims but more similar to other fellow-Europeans. There is an implication (since even European Muslims cannot easily escape Euro-centrism) that this new model would be somehow superior to other varieties, and may one day displace them. However, the emphasis at the moment is more on autonomy than hegemony.

The more ambitious North American claims are concerned more with hegemony than autonomy. Autonomy is a starting point, to be sure, as the aim is precisely to do away with the circularity of dependence on traditional religious authorities abroad in order to overcome the limitations of tradition. While some American Muslim intellectuals shy away from use of the "R" word,[26] others are not so hesitant in describing their endeavor in terms of an

"Islamic Reformation,"[27] indicating that the drive to build the "Second Mecca" out of the New Jerusalem is seriously under way.

There is, one has to say, nothing novel about modernizing and reformist Muslim intellectuals using the west as a launching pad for their reformist efforts. Activists have been doing this since the days of Sayyid Jamal al-Din al-Afghani (1837-1897). The leading "Euro-Islamist" (to coin a term), Tariq Ramadan, is himself the product of one such endeavor. His father, Said Ramadan, a leading figure in the Egyptian Muslim Brotherhood, came to Switzerland in the 1950's to escape persecution in his homeland. He established the Islamic Centre in Geneva both to continue his activism and also to propagate Islam in Europe in what he had hoped would be temporary exile. Europe and the US continue to be home to thriving Islamic communities and to movements forced into exile. So much so that claims are being made that the centre of gravity of such groups as the Muslim Brotherhood has shifted to Europe.[28] However, it is a great leap from acknowledging the fact that the West offers a more hospitable space for conducting traditional Islamic activism to arguing that it also offers the space for a novel kind of activism that is now transforming Islam itself.

As a matter of fact, a large segment of the exiled or immigrant Muslim activists continues to represent an extension of the thinking and concerns of their home movements. The centers which they set up in the West, such as the Islamic Foundation in Leicester, UK, or IIIT in the US, are closely linked to trends within the wider Muslim world. The myriad lobbying groups and other organizations set up in the US or Europe also form an extension of home movements or trends. Where exceptions exist, such as the innovative and more liberal thinking of the Tunisian Ennahda movement, led by Sheikh Rachid al-Ghannoushi, who is currently in exile in London, this has also been a continuation of the movement's line before the period of exile. In many respects, the "Second Mecca" looks very much like the first one, for now at least.

THE NEO-TRADITIONALIST LEGACY OF WESTERN ISLAM

However, this is not the whole story. For there is also a history of original contributions from European and Western Muslims to Islamic thought, as well as early claims from Western-based Muslim thinkers to positions of intellectual leadership. Prominent among these thinkers was the British Marmaduke William Pickthall (1875-1936), who converted to Islam in 1914 and became a leading figure on the post-war Indian cultural and political scene, writing a famous translation of the Qur'an in the process. No less significant is the man who succeeded Pickthall as editor of the Hyderabad journal *Islamic Culture*, and tried to emulate his enterprise of Qur'anic translation: Muhammad Asad (1900-1992). An Austrian-born journalist who converted to Islam from Judaism in the 1920's, Asad lived in Saudi Arabia and the Indian subcontinent before moving to Spain in 1955. He acted as a close advisor to the Saudi King and later to the Pakistani government, which he served in many capacities, including as UN Ambassador.

Intellectually, Asad is the precursor of the dominant "neo-traditionalist"[29] trend among Western converts to Islam, who harbor a romantic admiration for the traditional virtues of pre-modern Muslim societies and are almost sorry to see it modernize. His first book, *Islam at the Crossroads* (1934), offered an uncompromising criticism of western modernity and its materialism and warned Muslims against following in its footsteps. It was heavily quoted by modern Islamist thinkers, something which later became a matter of regret for him. In an introduction to a new edition in 1982, and in a later essay (*This Law of Ours*, 1987), he expressed disappointment at the excessive literalism and fixation with medieval practices of the modern revivalist movements at the expense of the true spirit of Islam.[30] His writings, including his magisterial study/translation of the Qur'an (*The Message of the Qur'an*, 1980), provoked admiration as well as controversy. Traditionalists strongly criticized the Abduh-inspired rationalist approach he adopted in rendering the Qur'an into English, and leading Islamic institutions refused to endorse it.

However, many other sections of the Muslim community continue to admire and use his translation.

Asad's neo-traditionalism is being perpetuated by figures such as Abdul-Hakim Murad (1960-), a sufi-inspired British-born Muslim, who writes constantly in support of traditionalist moderation, and Asad's own disciple, Murad Wilfred Hoffman who stirred a controversy by expressing support in one of his books for chastizing the wife (albeit as a symbolic gesture whilst mentioning that the Prophet personally rejected any corporeal punishment of his wives) at a time when he was Germany's ambassador in Morocco in the early 1990's. Prominent in this category are also the two leading figures in the California-based Zaytuna Institute: Imam Hamza Yusuf (1960-) and Imam Zaid Shakir (1965-).

The inclination towards traditionalism among a significant sector of native European and American Muslims is due mainly to the fact that western converts have predominantly been attracted to Islam by the lure of its spiritualism and its pre-modern (not to say anti-modern) ethos, and tended to romanticize these characteristics. This trend is increasing both in numbers and influence, especially in the post-9/11 era, when it began to present itself as a more credible alternative to the now discredited or feared revivalist Islam.

Neo-traditionalism is also being promoted by Sufi-inspired authors such as George Washington University's Seyyed Hossein Nasr (1933-). Nasr, a respected Iranian-born scholar and prolific author,[31] was also forced into exile by the outbreak of the Iranian revolution in 1979. His sufi-inspired traditionalist and largely apolitical vision of a spiritually enriched moderate Islam has found receptive ears in the West, and more recently outside it.

The traditionalists' hostility to any accommodation with modernity was given a stark expression by Maryum Jameelah (1934-), a New Yorker who embraced Islam in the 1950's and moved to Pakistan where she still lives. Jameelah ascribes her attitude to her own upbringing in a Reformed Jewish family, an experience which proved to her that attempts to accommodate modernity are lethal for any religious tradition.

> Even before I formally embraced Islam, I found the integrity of the faith in the contemporary world greatly threatened by the so-called modernist movement which aimed at adulterating its teachings with man-made philosophies and reforms. I was convinced that had these modernizers had their way, nothing of the original would be left! ... Throughout my childhood, the intellectual dishonesty, hypocrisy and superficiality of "reformed" Judaism was a vivid experience. Even at that early age I knew that such a watered down, half-hearted compromise could never hope to retain the loyalty of its members, much less their children... How shocked I was when I found certain scholars and some political leaders within the Muslim community guilty of the identical sins for which the God in our Holy Qur'an has vehemently denounced the Jews![32]

A similar mistrust of modernity and modernists is expressed by Nasr, who argues that the Islamic and modernist visions are so diametrically opposed that "no amount of wishy-washy apologetics can harmonize the two."[33] But while Jameelah's ultra-traditionalism caused her to gravitate towards the revivalists, (Jamaat Islami's leader Abu'l-Ala Maududi in fact declared her a soul-mate even before they met), the prevalent attitude among neo-traditionalists is mistrust of Islamic revivalists and modernists "who are more eager to establish institutes for Islamic social sciences than to build seminaries."[34] These ethically challenged proponents of identity politics, the neo-traditionalists argue, are not the answer for Islam's crisis. They tend to instrumentalize religion and "to define themselves sociologically, rather than theologically." Their version of instrumentalized Islam is not only spiritually, but artistically and humanly impoverished and very narrowly partisan.

> God is not denied by the sloganeers of identity; rather He is enlisted as a party member. No such revivalist can entertain the suggestion that the new liberation being recommended is a group liberation in the world that marginalises the more fundamental project of an individual liberation from the world; but his vocabulary nonetheless steadily betrays him. In the Qur'an, the word iman (usually translated as 'faith') appears twenty times as frequently as the word islam. In the sermons of the identity merchants, the ratio usually seems to be reversed.[35]

The neo-traditionalists are equally critical of Muslim liberals, whose "thoroughgoing theological liberalism remains a friendless elite option."[36] The answer can neither be found in the laxness of the liberals nor the "anger, anxiety, fear, and rage" of the impatient zealots, but in the serenity, patience and saintly selflessness of true believers.[37]

THE REFORMISM OF RADICAL MODERNISTS

While the neo-traditionalists tend to emphasize the spiritual/ethical dimension of Islam, the more predominant type among western-based Muslim intellectuals is a reformer who believes that Islam needs more input from modernity, not less. Typically an exiled university don, his/her emphasis is on an intellectual reformulation and reinterpretation of the Islamic tradition so as to better accommodate the demands of modernity.

Modern Islamic revivalism (and even the modern manifestations of traditionalism) are nothing but a constant effort to come to terms with the social, political and intellectual challenges posed by modernity. The traditionalists try to make minimal concessions to modernity, just enough to preserve the maximum that could be preserved from tradition. But even here, tradition is being constantly redefined and reformulated. The revivalists are more aggressive when it comes to redefining the tradition, motivated as they are precisely by the worry that the tradition cannot be preserved as it stands. However, revivalists further distinguish themselves from the traditionalists by redefining the tradition into more hardline and purist terms than the former, who tend to accept the tradition more or less as it had been handed down. A third category, the modernists, also seeks to redefine the tradition along similar lines to the revivalists, but tends towards more liberal and accommodating interpretations of that tradition. Needless to say, there is plenty of overlap and interpenetration between these trends. Today's modernist could be tomorrow's traditionalist, while one could find traditionalists among revivalists or modernists, and vice versa.

The trend we would like to call here "radical modernism" has emerged as a reaction to what some analysts (and other critics, including revivalists and modernists) describe as the failure of Islamic modernism.[38] Radical modernism represents an attempt to advance the modernist project further by interrogating the tradition in more radical ways. Unlike the traditionalists, who favor the preservation of inherited tradition as it had been handed down the centuries, or the revivalists who want to displace the inherited tradition with what they see as the more authentic and uncorrupted teachings of Islam, the radical modernists question both the living tradition and the proposed "authentic" alternatives. The early generation of modernists did not go this far, seeking merely to exploit the differences and conflicts within orthodoxy itself to eliminate or discredit those aspects of the tradition which have become difficult to sell or defend in the modern era. They selectively pick and choose from various accepted authorities in order to support their modernizing (usually liberal) agenda. The radical modernists go further, arguing that the authentic sources have actually been misunderstood by successive generations of Muslims, and need to be understood in radically new ways.

Among the influential figures in this category was the Algerian born Malik Bennabi (1905-1973), who lived in France between 1930 and 1954 before moving to Cairo and then to independent Algeria in 1962 where he worked for a time as Director of Higher Education. Bennabi is regarded as the inspiration behind the dominant faction in the Front Islamique de Salut (FIS) which won the aborted elections of 1991. But he himself was concerned less with specific religious thought and more with the "conditions of renaissance" (a title of one of his books) and wrote extensively about the need for a revival of an authentic Muslim civilization through intellectual and spiritual regeneration. In this, his work has parallels with that of another French-educated Muslim intellectual, the Iranian Ali Shariati (1933-1977) who studied in France in the 1960's and was also credited with a critical role in inspiring the Islamic revolution in Iran. Both concentrated on analysing the crisis of the Muslim civilization in almost Weberian terms, and avoided direct discussions of Islamic doctrine, except when examining its potential for civilizational regeneration.

Shariati's brief exile to London lasted only three weeks, ending tragically with his assassination 1977. But his legacy is being perpetuated by a host of exiled or marginalized Iranian intellectuals. Foremost amongst these is the philosopher-activist Abdolkarim Soroush (1945-), who challenges the living tradition by distinguishing between religion, which is absolute and transcendental, and religious knowledge, which is always relative and context-dependent. He uses this distinction to critique traditional interpretations of religious doctrines in favor of a more liberal and pluralistic stance.[39] Soroush has a strong influence among students and young activists in Iran and beyond, but he was forced by regime harassment to spend more time working and teaching in the US and Europe.

However, the epitome of the Islamic intellectual in exile has to be the late Pakistani-American Oxford-educated Fazlur Rahman (1919-1988), who has made important contributions to Islamic scholarship and modern Islamic thought, mainly from his post as professor at the University of Chicago. Typical also is the fact that Fazlur Rahman was not in the US by choice, having been forced to abandon his position as Director of the Central Institute of Islamic Research and as advisor to the President of Pakistan on Islamic affairs (1962-1968) because of the controversy surrounding his views on reform. In particular, Rahman stirred intense anger among the traditionalists by propounding a skeptical view of the status of the Prophet's hadith (sayings), and a more "humanist" view of revelation. The "downgrading" of the authority of hadith in favor of the Qur'an has been a persistent theme among modern reformists seeking to undermine the dogmatic hold of tradition. But the strategy usually met with fierce and effective opposition from the traditionalists. However, Fazlur Rahman went even further by arguing that the Qur'an itself was not purely divine, but incorporated a significant human input from the Prophet.[40] This approach is similar to the one advocated by Nasr Abu Zayd (of whom more below), and the result in both cases was similar: an intensely hostile reaction from the religious establishment.

The fact that Fazlur Rahman found it difficult even to remain in Pakistan, let alone build up a following there, is typical of many leading Muslim intellectuals whose main problem was not only harassment by despotic regimes, but hostility from the masses swayed by traditional religious scholars. In other words, it is usually losing the struggle for religious authority to the *ʿulamā'* and other traditionalists which sends them into exile, thus undermining their very claim of representing an alternative voice of religious authority. Equally typically, Fazlur Rahman threw his lot in with an "enlightened despot," in this case the military ruler Ayoub Khan, in the hope of pushing reform from above. This was a strategy adopted from as long back as the era of the rationalist Muʿtazilites, who teamed up with the Abbasid Caliph al-Ma'mūn (198/813-218/833) to push their rationalist agenda through state power, and ended up as one of the few major Islamic sects that had become completely extinct.

Choosing exile under these circumstances appeared to be an admission of defeat and a sign of despair. Exile in the West further undermines the effectiveness of reformers, especially given that the pressures and demands of integration into Western academia weaken the claims of these intellectuals to religious authority even further.[41] One has to travel (as Fazlur Rahman did) a long way – literally and figuratively – from *Dar al-ʿUlūm* in Deoband to the University of Chicago in order to achieve prominence in one of the major shrines of Western secular academia. And this two-dimensional distance greatly reduces the impact of the message being "beamed back" to the rest of the Muslim world.

Fazlur Rahman and other leading Muslim intellectuals in the West, including two of his close associates, Ismail Raji al-Faruqi (1921-1986) and Seyyed Hossein Nasr, did have some (posthumous in the case of both Rahman and Faruqi) impact on the wider Muslim intellectual scene. This happened mainly through their students and publications. Nasr's ideas have found a fertile ground in countries like Indonesia, where his works have been translated and adopted by influential figures.[42] Two of Fazlur Rahman's students became leading lights on the Indonesian Islamic scene, and he is cited as a key influence on the rising trend of Indonesian "Islamic liberalism."[43] However, it has to be noted that what had been decisive in this instance was the adoption of their work by embattled predominantly home-grown movements that started looking around in search of intellectual support for their stance.

In what could be a sign of the times, one of Fazlur Rahman's leading associates, al-Faruqi, who tried to make a virtue out of the plight of exile, appeared to have shifted back decisively towards a more traditional modernist/revivalist stance. Palestinian-born Ismail al-Faruqi, has worked with Fazlur Rahman as a visiting professor of Islamic studies and scholar-in-residence at McGill University in the late 1950's before accompanying him to Pakistan. Differences between the two close colleagues led Faruqi to return early to a professorship at Temple University where he was later joined by Nasr.

In 1981, Faruqi founded the International Institute of Islamic Thought (IIIT), an enterprise which embodied his ideal of promoting an Islamic renaissance based on the appropriation of modern knowledge via an Islamic framework. The "Islamization of knowledge" project was seen as simultaneously a quest for an intellectual and civilizational revival and a reclamation of Islamic authenticity.[44] Relying on generous funding from private Saudi sources, the project mobilized the talents and efforts of hundreds of Western-based Muslim scholars, and continues to organize a vast network of scholars and institutions from its Virginia headquarters and its twelve regional offices around the world.

Faruqi was murdered in mysterious circumstances in 1986 together with his wife while still working at Temple. However, in the 1980's some of IIIT's key figures were tasked with setting up the International Islamic University in Kuala Lumpur in order to advance the project further. Faruqi's legacy is currently being carried on by people like Iraqi-born Taha J. Alalwani (1935-), the Saudi-born AbdulHamid AbuSulayman, and members of the Association of American Muslim Social Scientists (and similar associations in Europe and around the world).

The tradition inaugurated by Fazlur Rahman lives on in the work of a new generation of intellectuals who similarly have hit a wall in their attempts to promote reform at home and moved to Europe or the US instead. In what looked like a supreme irony, Ebrahim Moosa, the editor of his posthumous work (*Revival and Reform in Islam*)[45] had himself lived through an identical experience which forced him to temporarily flee his home in South Africa to seek refuge in Chicago.

Similar work is being carried out by the Islamic Centre of Southern California (ICSC), founded by the Egyptian-born brothers Hassan and Maher Hathout. One key figure affiliated with the Centre is Dr Fathi Osman (1928-), an Egyptian-born scholar and writer who edited a magazine in London in the 1980's before moving to California.[46] In this category one can include Swiss-born Tariq Ramadan, whose recent call for a "moratorium" on Islamic punishments stirred fierce controversy, and the late Zaki Badawi (1922-2006), the Egyptian-born British Muslim leader whose advice to British Muslim women to abandon the hijab to avoid harassment in the aftermath of the 7/7 bombings in London provoked a heated debate in the summer of 2005. Other groups such as the City Circle (a group of young Muslim professionals) in London, have also emerged with the explicit purpose of helping the new Muslim generation to evolve new ways of thinking better adapted to life in the West. Similar groups, such as the "Radical Middle Way" circle (centered around the London-based youth-oriented Muslim magazine *Q-News*) or the Islamic Society of Britain, also attempt to achieve the same objectives using slightly different approaches.

What unites the intellectual figures and schools within this trend of radical modernism is an approach which seeks to work within the confines of orthodoxy, while working hard to redefine it. They attempt to develop a radical re-reading and re-interpretation of traditional Islamic sources by adapting traditionally approved approaches and methods of interpretation, even though they often come up with readings which the religious establishment finds difficult to accept.

This accentuates the predicament of these radical modernists, who are forced to wage battle on two fronts simultaneously: in defense of Islam against external attacks, and in defense of their own "modernized" understanding of Islam against the guardians of tradition. In order not to be thoroughly isolated, they often have to choose which primary battle to wage: a war for Islam against its western detractors (the apparent choice of Tariq Ramadan and the Southern California group) in which one is careful not to antagonize the guardians of tradition, or a war for modernism against its traditional opponents (the apparent choice of Fazlur Rahman) where you keep the secular and western allies on board. Usually, these intellectuals get the worst of both worlds, being rejected by both the traditionalists and their secular opponents, which is also the fate of many among the even more radical reformists to whom we will turn in a moment.

What distinguishes radical modernists is their preference to waging their primary battle against the traditionalists, since their central argument is that without a radical rethinking of tradition Islam will not be able to survive modernity and Muslim societies will continue to lag behind other societies. Some of them are more cautious in their approach than others, but all are more careful than the next category of ultra-radical modernists when it comes to antagonizing the traditionalists.

It is thus a supreme irony that some of these thinkers (such as Bennabi and Shariati) appear to have inspired movements that were much more dogmatic than they would have liked, even though they have also helped inspire more open-minded movements, as we have also seen. Of no less significance is the way in which evolution within Islamic thought in the West has also witnessed other important shifts. The odyssey of the "Ijmali" group of intellectuals (based in the UK but also operating in the US, Europe and Malaysia), illustrates this trajectory. Vividly chronicled by one of its leading lights, Zia Sardar, in his recent autobiographical work *Desperately Seeking Paradise* (2005), this group emerged within the broader exiled Islamic movement but soon began to outgrow it. Working within organizations such as the Federation of Student Islamic Societies (FOSIS) in the UK and similar organizations, members were influenced by groups such as the traditionalist Tablighi Jamaat before gravitating towards Islamist groups such the Muslim Brotherhood and Jamaat Islami. They began to work in Saudi-funded institutions in the oil boom era before shifting their allegiance to Islamic Iran which began to fund their publications and think tanks. In the end, they became disillusioned with both Islamism and Muslim regimes and went back to the drawing board, seeking to start from where figures such as Fazlur Rahman have ended.

ULTRA-RADICAL MODERNISTS

For a new emerging breed of Muslim intellectuals, the radical modernism of Fazlur Rahman and similar intellectuals was too timid and conventional. These "ultra-radical modernists" have taken a conscious decision to launch a frontal attack on traditionalism, as was done by the Egyptian scholar, Nasr Hamid Abu Zayd, who stirred controversy by his book *The Concept of the Text* (1990), in which he advocated treating the Qur'an as a "human" text and using the tools of modern literary criticism to decipher it. Abu Zayd fled Egypt to Holland in 1995 after a court declared him an apostate and decreed a forcible divorce from his wife.

Abu Zayd sums up his position on contextualizing the Qur'an as follows:

> For Muslim scholars, the Qur'an was always a text from the moment of its canonization until the present moment. Yet, if we pay close attention to the Qur'an as discourse or discourses, it is no longer sufficient to re-contextualize one or more passages in the fight against literalism and fundamentalism, or against a specific historical practice that seems inappropriate for our modern context. Similarly, it is not enough to invoke modern hermeneutics to justify the historicity and hence the relativity of every mode of understanding, while in the meantime claiming that our modern interpretation is more appropriate and more valid. What these inadequate approaches produce is either polemic or apologetic hermeneutics.

> Without rethinking the Qur'an and without re-invoking its living status as a reformation of Islamic thought 'discourse', whether in academia or in everyday life, democratic and open hermeneutics cannot be achieved...
>
> To reconnect the question of the meaning of the Qur'an to that of the meaning of life, it is now imperative to note that the Qur'an was the outcome of dialogue, debate, argument, acceptance and rejection, both with pre-Islamic norms, practices and culture, and with its own previous assessments, presuppositions and assertions.[47]

In a similar position is Emory University's Abdullahi Ahmed An-Na'im, a law professor who advocates a liberal interpretation of Islam that would make it compatible with international human rights. Sudanese-born An-Na'im bases his ideas on the sufi-inspired insights of his mentor, the late Mahmud Muhammad Taha, who was executed for heresy in Sudan in 1985, an act which outraged large sections of opinion inside and outside Sudan. This sets him apart from the bulk of modernists who rely on rational arguments, rather than essentially religious (in this case mystical) insights, to back their reformist agendas. Taha's main tool was "reverse abrogation," the argument that earlier sections of the Qur'an from the Makkan period, which emphasize mainly general values, should supersede the later ones which give detailed legal and personal instructions.[48]

Also a key figure in this category is UCLA's Law Professor Khaled Abou El Fadl (1963-), a prominent and prolific liberal scholar. Kuwaiti-born Abou El Fadl epitomizes the dilemmas of reformist Islamic thinkers in the West. Described somewhat hyperbolically by his supporters on a dedicated website as "the most important and influential Islamic thinker in the modern age," he has been attacked by some western critics as a "stealth Islamist,"[49] and described by some fellow liberal Muslims as an advocate of "a dictatorship of Muslim jurists."[50] He has also drawn a wave of criticisms (and even death threats) from some quarters in response to his criticisms of the Muslim response to the 9/11 attacks and his frequent diatribes against Wahhabi conservatives. His theses on Islam and democracy were rejected by some Islamists as coming from "outside" the Islamic perspective, and were thus "hard to swallow" for Muslims.[51]

In his work, Abou El Fadl uses his grounding in traditional Islamic sciences and expertise in modern jurisprudence to advocate a modernity-friendly interpretation of Islamic doctrine opposed to the more strict one espoused by radicals or traditionalists. Like Fazlur Rahman, his main tool is to query the faithfulness of traditional interpretations to the true spirit of Islam, mainly through questioning the authenticity of the bulk of the body of hadith, and through attacks on what he sees as rigid Wahhabi scripturalism.[52] His diligent quest for that elusive magical formula of faithfulness to tradition and full embracing of modernity ends, however, in angering both traditionalists and modernists alike. He often undermines his own logic, as when he tries to privilege context over text in his analyses, as when he argues that the exultation of the virtue of sacrifice among early Muslims was a contingent measure dictated by the state of siege under which Muslims lived at the time.[53] However, his opponents could (and do) argue, using the same logic of contingency, that these values are doubly relevant today, precisely because the Ummah is under siege as never before. So even if traditional Islamic values did not support militancy, a militant response becomes imperative because of the unprecedented wave of foreign aggression.

Abou El Fadl is a founding member of a group calling itself "Progressive Muslims," an informal grouping which began to take form in the post-9/11 climate in the US. Its members founded the Progressive Union of North America (PMUNA) in late 2004, and began to run a number of websites, including Muslimwakeup.com and pmuna.org. The principles it advocates are summed up in belief in the equality of the worth of human life and of all human beings regardless of gender or religion, plus the espousal of social justice, gender equality and pluralism. The group also takes an anti-imperialist stance and moderate leftist positions on international issues.[54] Additionally, PMUNA espouses secularism and takes a liberal and tolerant social stance, most controversially with regards to homosexuality. But it distinguishes itself from other secular groups in actively seeking to base its stance on credibly authentic interpretations of the basic Islamic sources.

Among the key figures in the PMUNA is Omid Safi of Colgate University in the State of New York, and American-born Amina Wadud, Professor of Islamic Studies at Virginia Commonwealth University, who in March 2005 became the first woman to lead a mixed sex congregation in Friday prayers. Wadud is author of *Qur'an and Woman: Rereading the Sacred Text from A Woman's Perspective* (1999), a bold attempt at legitimizing feminist positions from an Islamic perspective.

Wadud's "gender jihad" is joined by a number of equally combative American Muslim women activists, including Aziza al-Hibri, Asra Nomani and Asma Barlas. One can add here as well the Canadian Irshad Manji, an openly lesbian young writer advocating radical reform that should jettison traditional authoritarianism in favor of a more enlightened and tolerant faith. It is, it has been argued, the robust contribution of these gender-jihadists to the debate – and activism – (including the active campaign to end male monopoly of control over places of worship) which gives American Islamic reform activism its distinctive character.[55]

Among the founders of PMUNA also is University of Maryland's Muqtader Khan, whose website (ijtihad.org) and prolific works seek to propagate a message of moderate, pro-western democracy-friendly interpretation of Islam. His views frequently draw harsh criticisms from more radical or traditionalist Muslim activists who accuse him of being too pro-establishment. Khan's inclusion among those invited to join the founders of PMUNA at its inception in November 2004 was cited by dissident "progressive Muslims" as evidence that the group was not progressive enough, opting to include pro-establishment figures, or even some with "impeccable imperialist credentials" among its founders. As a consequence, this dissident group declined to join the forum and published a letter outlining the grounds for its objections.[56]

In July 2005, however, Khan resigned from the Advisory Board of PMUNA, alleging that the group did not observe the principles of tolerance, pluralism and democracy it advocated and treated those who disagreed with the dominant views within the group with disdain and disrespect. In his letter of resignation, Khan also alleged that the group was disrespectful of Islamic teachings and sources and had been gratuitously abusive towards mainstream American Muslim groups and community leaders.[57]

Khan's remarks echo criticisms made against PMUNA by other Muslim groups inside and outside the US. Before his resignation, Khan also criticized PMUNA's style and some of its initiatives, including Wadud's Friday prayers move, which he alleged were divisive and tended to alienate the very audience the progressives sought to influence. The group, he complained, undermines the cause of progressive Muslims by showing indifference to, even ignorance of, core Islamic teachings, and would do well to be more tolerant and less abusive towards its opponents.[58]

The squabbling within the "progressive Muslims" camp is indicative of the fragility of this project and its tentative character. It also greatly undermines its moral authority and its wider impact. However, the main limitation of the group, as one key member put it, is its inability to extricate itself from the hegemonistic agenda of the dominant western discourse. The demands of "living inside an imperial power" and "being part of the imperialism" poses to the group "the critical questions" of "who is defining the issues, and where are the answers coming from?"[59]

The rise of the ultra-radical trend is a response to a perceived crisis within radical modernism in the same way as the latter trend emerged in response to crises within revivalism and early modernism. The squabbles within the movement also reflects similar dilemmas to those experienced by the radical modernists who found it difficult to break completely with the paradigm and methodology of revivalism. The criticism of being "disrespectful" of Islamic teachings levelled against the progressives from within their ranks points to an attachment to some of the tenets of the radical modernists who were careful to protest their respect for tradition and faithfulness to it. This is also further evidence of continuing overlap between these competing trends, which seek to displace one another, but are also keen on preserving some key characteristics of their rivals.

THE LIMITATIONS OF REFORM FROM EXILE

From this brief outline one can see that the contribution of western Muslims to the cause of Islamic revival and renewal, or the use of the West as a refuge by reformers fleeing persecution, is not a new phenomenon. However, what is new and significant is the increased boldness and progressive radicalization of successive generations of western-based Muslim intellectuals. Traditionalists (and neo-traditionalists) are no longer vying only with the radical modernists, who sought to evolve a creative synthesis of tradition and modern ideas, and faced criticism from both sides. They have also to fight a contest with the increasingly bold "progressives" and other ultra-radical modernists who are less concerned about preserving tradition than in transcending it. The more irreverent and iconoclastic progressives are not afraid of openly defying mainstream orthodoxy or deliberately courting controversy. They are ready to go well beyond the current limits of orthodoxy by arguing for positions which unapologetically advocate a break with tradition in such areas as gay relationships, complete gender equality and the opposition to many Islamic legal sanctions.

One has to take care not to confuse the ultra-radical "reformists" with another tendency among secular academics who make important criticisms of religious thought, but without putting forth claims of representing an alternative religious view of their own. Among this group we can count Algerian-born Professor Muhammad Arkoun of the Sorbonne in Paris, Syrian-born Bassam Tibi of the University of Goettingen in Germany, and his fellow countryman Aziz Al-Azmeh, who currently teaches in Budapest. While these authors, and in particular Arkoun, hope to see their views heeded by the religiously inclined, their contributions are not specifically directed at the believing masses or intelligentsia. Like their western academic counterparts, their aim is to improve understanding of religious thought rather than to contribute to it. One can liken this group to sports coaches, who would offer a lot of advice to potential athletes, but would rather not do any sprinting themselves.

What is also novel is the increased receptiveness to the ideas of western-based thinkers in the wider Muslim world. Their influence has grown in recent years and become the focus of attention in the media and within western and Muslim intellectual circles, largely due to the glare of publicity these contributions generated in the post-September 11 climate. In this "post-Islamist" era (to use a term coined by Leiden University's Asef Bayat), characterized by disillusionment about Islamic revivalism and its promises,[60] their role has come into prominence. As the clamoring for "reform" reaches fever pitch in official (and semi-official) policy circles both in the West and in major Muslim countries, the demand for the input of these intellectuals exponentially increases. Both Western and Muslim governments have made the promotion of a more "moderate" Islam to counter various forms of radicalism a priority. Major research institutions in the West also encourage work in this area. An endless stream of works on themes such as "liberal Islam," "Islamic liberalism," "Islamic Reformation," etc., is now being churned by printing presses the world over. There is also, in addition, a genuine grass roots demand for alternative visions of Islam to replace the discredited extremist or revivalist schemas now being shunned by an increasing number of disillusioned individuals and sectors. In responding to this multi-faceted demand for change, some intellectual figures and movements tend to deploy more aggressive tactics, establishing new institutions and cultivating new alliances with influential movements and political leaders. Others are content with the usual methods of writing, lecturing and cultivating students and followers.

According to some analysts, both the role and the challenge facing Muslim intellectuals in the West is connected with the "deterritorialization of culture" where cultures become delinked from their geographic moorings.[61] However, it is not merely the delinkage of territory and culture which is the issue here, but the delinkage of culture and power. Muslim communities in the West lack the capability dominant communities have to use power to protect their cultural norms or enforce them. Again this is not a novel feature in religious traditions, as it had been the fate of Christianity in its first four centuries and it had been the fate of Judaism for over two millennia. But it has been very rare for those sections of the community living in exile to significantly influence those sections which combine cultural authority and power from their external position. Tensions between political power and religious authority are behind the major transformations and schisms which affected Christianity throughout its history, including the Reformation and subsequent secularization, both of which represented the tendency of political power to assert its autonomy vis-à-vis extra-territorial forces.

One of the major hurdles facing the contributions of Western Muslims therefore stem from their attempt to bring about a radical transformation in an established and very powerful religious tradition from a position which lacks both direct power and charismatic religious authority. However, even when they succeed, such attempts at religious transformation are potentially very divisive. Many analysts (who include Muslim activists and potential reformers) never cease to speak, with a quasi-messianic anticipation, of an awaited "Islamic reformation." However, these authors tend to forget two important points: first, that a "reformation" cannot be made to order, and in particular not to specifications conceived from outside the religious tradition in question; and, second, any radical rethinking of religion, even when it claims, as the Reformation (and modern Islamic revivalism) did, to hearken back to the more authentic roots of the religious tradition, is usually a prelude to a prolonged religious conflict.[62]

More important, the reform input must credibly aim to strengthen and revitalize religion, not to overtly advertise its intentions to dilute it and tailor it to secular demands conceived in from a rival religious tradition. The Luthers and Calvins of this world were no faint-hearted liberals seeking to "modernize" Christianity. Had that been their rallying call, it would have been ridiculously easy for the Catholic establishment to dismiss their claims. However, even then their input has been very divisive. The efforts of the secular-inspired

Muslim reformers are much easier to discredit and potentially even more divisive.

And to be sure, the claims of "Euro-Islam," even when advocated by "halal" Islamic scholars and activists, continue to stir angry reactions from, radicals, traditionalists and neo-traditionalists. The ultra-radical Hizb ut-Tahrir (Liberation Party) led the offensive, charging proponents of Euro-Islam with having succumbed to pressure from western governments that have "embarked on a new project, [in] which via coercion, and intimidation they plan to integrate the Muslims and force them to reform Islam" in order to contain the "Islamic threat."[63] Ramadan's call for a moratorium on Islamic punishments, and his casual remarks about the freedom of his children to marry non-Muslims, provoked a volley of angry outbursts from more traditionalist Muslims.

Overall, these potential reformers face a problem of credibility and authority. Part of the problem is inherent in the very structure of their endeavor. Western Muslim intellectuals face a dual challenge. To make their mark, they first have to ascend the academic ladder in Western establishments, which means that they have to establish their credentials in a secular agnostic environment. However, in order to establish their credentials as reformers, they have also to prove their Islamic authenticity and devotion to their religious tradition. To the extent that their work appeals to the Western academic establishment, on which their reputation, not to say their livelihood, depends, it tends to fall short of satisfying the requirements of authoritative Islamic impact.

It is to be recalled that many of these thinkers are fugitives who failed even to build a sufficiently strong following to enable them to find protection in numbers at home. Merely changing one's place of residence is not going to make his or her arguments more convincing, or give their opinions more weight. What is at issue is producing authoritative reinterpretations of the tradition which would be found convincing by a wide section of the Muslim public. And this requires an engagement in serious and intensive dialogue with the community. It also requires the possession of a considerable spiritual and moral authority acknowledged by the community.

The spiritual impoverishment of various strands of modernist reformism is accentuated and highlighted by the contrast with the more intensely spiritualist approach of the neo-traditionalists, who appear to have a monopoly on that aspect of religiosity. However, the spirituality of the traditionalists is combined, as we have seen, with an intense (and absurdly impractical) hostility to all things modern. By contrast, the crass political pragmatism (not to say the Machiavellianism) of the revivalists and most modernists (as evidenced by how easy they struck deals with dictators and other unsavory allies) and the pedantic intellectualism of the bulk of the radical and ultra-radical modernists, is not exactly the stuff of religious charisma.

As things stand now, these intellectuals are facing difficulties in interacting with the wider Muslim community even in the relative freedom and permissiveness of the West. Abou El Fadl, for example, reveals that he is no longer welcome at his local mosque in Southern California, and expresses despair about ever achieving recognition for his work in his lifetime. Observers regard him as an "isolated figure" even among American Muslims due to his sharp criticisms of mainstream groups.[64]

Abou El Fadl, like other figures in Western Muslim reformism, ascribes his lack of efficacy to problems of outreach and dissemination. His books are banned in most Muslim countries, and his calendar is not exactly cluttered with invitations to lecture in Muslim capitals. This, Abou El-Fadl and his colleagues argue, is due to the inordinate influence of conservative groups and governments, in particular the Saudi Wahhabi establishment, which does not like what they preach.

However, this problem of outreach is only one side of the problem. For if someone like Abou El-Fadl is not being found convincing, even at his local mosque, expanding his readership may not change things that much as far as the receptiveness to his ideas is concerned. In fact, one of the problems of many reformists may be that the discredited regimes and the mistrusted West have of late been overenthusiastic in promoting them and their ideas.

There is, in addition, the institutional problem. Most of the prominent figures in the western reformist movements and trends function as isolated individuals embedded into mainstream institutions, or as members of informal groupings. But in spite of attempts to build up representative institutions for Muslims in the West, no credible *religious* institutions or seminaries have been set up to rival the major seminaries operating within the Muslim world. And this in spite of the fact that those institutions did not enjoy any impressive credibility to start with. The institutional weakness in this area is another reflection of the general spiritual underdevelopment of the reformist movement as a whole. However, this may change with the attention the otherwise university-bound intellectuals are beginning to pay to religious institutions and other aspects of religious practice.

Add to this that, in spite of claims (cited above) to the contrary, Muslim communities do not yet enjoy the financial and institutional independence they crave (or boast of) vis-à-vis the wider Muslim world. Most of the active groups speaking for Muslims in Europe and the US, while embracing a wide spectrum of views, continue to represent a direct extension of movements and trends at home, while many are indirectly inspired by home trends. The structure of funding for Islamic institutions and organizations, which often comes directly from governments (in particular the Gulf monarchies and Iran) or from private sources with a religious agenda, determines the orientation of these groups. The views expressed within the "mainstream" range from the largely orthodox, even conservative inclination of institutions or groups affiliated to Islamist groups or to the religious establishments in various countries, to the relatively more liberal trends mentioned above. Espousing some form of orthodox revivalism, these groups are unlikely, given this inclination, to have a radical earth shattering impact on Muslim communities back home.

CONCLUSION

ARE western Muslims then an endangered species, or are they the future of Islam? They are certainly a long way from being either, even if they seem to be attempting to turn their precarious status into a virtue. The accelerated adaptation and change western Muslims are pushed to make in order just to survive has galvanized them into a serious effort of rethinking and reflection. This has, in turn, moved the worldwide debate on Islamic reform into a new higher gear.

However, the very nature of the pressures western Muslims face, and the direction in which they are required to adapt, is the very opposite of that demanded by religious reform. Pressures from outside demand the downplaying of any particular religious specificity or commitment, and require more the listening and adapting to voices coming from outside the particular religious tradition. But genuine religious reform must come from a very different impulse: an impulse towards a deeper commitment to, and an urge to enhance and elevate, the particular religious experience. It depends on listening more, and more intensely, to the voice from the inside (both from within the heart and from within the community) rather than the voices coming from without.

Discussions of the Christian Reformation tend to confuse scholarly analyses based on hindsight with the real intentions of the leaders of the Reformation. The fact that the Reformation is seen from our perspective (with hindsight) as having contributed to the dilution of religious commitment, and accelerated secularization and the disintegration of the religious universe, does not mean that this had been the intention of its initiators. In fact the leaders of the Reformation were passionate, even fanatical, proponents of even stricter religious observance than their rivals. Reaction to their proposals would have been even more drastic had they called for the "liberalization" or "modernization" of Christianity or (horror of horrors!) rapprochement with Judaism or Islam!

A religious reform project which seeks to bring about the unintended consequences of the Reformation while neglecting its ethos is to misunderstand the very nature of religious authority. This is a great irony for authors like Abou El Fadl who had dedicated so much effort to the study of the nature and dynamics of religious authority. But in any case such a deliberate drive for a "reformation" based on copying another experience, from another era, in another religious tradition, is condemned from the start to the loss of innocence: it is no longer religious reform, but social engineering and intellectual tinkering.

The difficulties faced by some of the key intellectual figures among Western Muslims sum up the predicament of these would-be reformers. Just as Abou El Fadl continues to feel isolated and persecuted, more "orthodox" figures like Ramadan, also face similar hostility from all directions: branded by secular and western intellectuals as closet militants, and dismissed by traditionalists as "instruments of the cultural imperialism." The French intellectual-politician Bernard Kouchner described Ramadan as "the most dangerous man in Europe," while Bernard-Henri Levy dubbed him "the intellectual champion of all kinds of double-talk."[65] His visa to the US was revoked without explanation in the summer of 2004, preventing him from taking a professorship at the University of Notre Dame, and effectively categorizing him as a terror threat. On the other side, one typical Arab commentator described his call for a moratorium on Islamic punishments as an irrelevant and suspect move, based on superficial arguments and faulty and deficient religious knowledge.[66]

The lack of popularity among Muslim audiences is not a problem in itself, since religious reformers always face an uphill task at the start. However, this isolation becomes a problem if it persists and begins to resemble a cul-de-sac. It is interesting to note that even initiatives which enjoyed a fair measure of legitimacy, such as IIIT's Islamization of Knowledge project, have yet to make the anticipated decisive impact. The ethos of the IK project was to reconstitute the disciplines of modern knowledge in light of Islamic precepts of knowledge to a) renegotiate the terms set by the global encounter and reclaim the Islamic consciousness which had become submerged under modes of thought set by the West and b) develop a critical and objective reassessment of the Western mind. Given the scale of the work involved and the challenges that lay ahead it is not surprising that a quarter of a century and millions of dollars later, the desired breakthrough of a Muslim intellectual and cultural revival has on certain levels not been realized.[67]

A distinct brand of "Euro-Islam" or "American Islam" may well evolve and ultimately succeed in reconciling Islam with western democracy and secularism. But for this brand of Islam to drive rival brands out of business, and not merely turn into a new fringe sect, it needs to tap into resources of religious authority which the spokespersons of this movement do not yet enjoy.

Of great significance in this regard is the problematic status of the African-American Muslim community, probably the single largest bloc of native western Muslims. African-American Islam had a strong political component, an aspect which put it in conflict with orthodoxy in its early phases. Far from vying for leadership politically and intellectually, African-American Islam is still recovering from its early isolationist and racialist phase, while African-American Muslims continue to complain from a double marginalization: within America and within the Muslim community.[68] But the community is producing some of the key protagonists in the current debate on reform, and can make an important difference by lending its weight to this or that side in it.

Western-based Muslim intellectuals might derive some momentary satisfaction from the fact that their writings are increasingly being read, translated, quoted and debated in the wider *Dar al-Islam*. But the question they have to answer is this: are they being quoted and listened to because they are westerners or because they are

Muslims? I have a suspicion that Karl Popper (and the other Karl) are being quoted in Iran more frequently and with more approval than Abdolkarim Soroush.[69] It is one thing to be regarded as a charismatic source of religious authority, and another to be seen as just an alternative to Habermas.

In order to have an impact in the *religious* sphere, as these intellectuals aspire, then they have to be more than just "intellectuals." And that may be a big hurdle to jump over. Intellectuals cannot, after all, help but be just that: *intellectuals*.

NOTES

1 Tomas Gerholm, "Two Muslim Intellectuals in the postmodern West: Akbar Ahmed and Ziauddin Sardar," in Akbar Ahmed and Hastings Donnan, eds., *Islam, Globalization and Postmodernity* (London: Routledge, 1994), p.191.
2 Ibid., p.207
3 Ibid., p.206.
4 Murad Hoffman, "Islamic Renaissance in the West: An Interview with Murad Hoffman" (in Hossam Tammam) *IslamOnline.net*, 15 January 2004 (accessed November 29, 2005). http://www.islamonline.net/english/ArtCulture/2004/01/article07.html. (Accessed August 20, 2005).
5 Jocelyne Cesari, *When Islam and Democracy Meet: Muslims in Europe and the United States* (New York: Palgrave Macmillan, 2004), p.173.
6 Osman Bakar, "The Intellectual Impact of American Muslim Scholars on the Muslim World, with Special Reference to Southeast Asia," a paper of The Center for Muslim-Christian Understanding (Georgetown University, June 2003), pp.1-2. http://cmcu.georgetown.edu/PDFs/Intellectual_impact_of_American_Muslim_scholars.pdf. (Accessed November 13, 2005).
7 Tammam, "Islamic Renaissance in the West."
8 Cesari, *When Islam and Democracy Meet*, p.165.
9 The publication in 1988 of Rushdie's novel *The Satanic Verses*, has elicited numerous protests (some violent) in the UK and worldwide because of perceived insults to the Prophet Muhammad and his family. This was the first major confrontation in which the Muslim community in Britain acted collectively in sharp opposition to the mainstream stance which found it difficult to understand or sympathize with Muslim grievances in this regard, seeing Muslim demands as contradicting the core values of freedom of speech and religious belief. See Tariq Modood, "British Asian Muslims and the Rushdie Affair," *The Political Quarterly* (1990), vol. 62, no. 2, pp.143-160. Cf. Pnina Werbner, "Diaspora and Millennium: British Pakistani

Global-Local Fabulations of the Gulf War," in Ahmed and Donnan, *Islam, Globalisation and Postmodernity*, pp.213-236.

10 Werbner describes the Rushdie affair as a "watershed" in the evolution of the British Muslim community (Werbner, "Diaspora and Millennium," p.231).

11 Among the most celebrated intellectual who took this detour are Fay Weldon (Britain) a novelist who became Salman Rushdie's most ardent supporter from 1989 and a fierce critic of Islam and Muslims. Others include British-born Christopher Hitchens (US) and Paul Berman (US).

12 Abdal-Hakim Murad "European Islam: the return of Hagar," *open Democracy*, 3 July 2003. www.opendemocracy.net/debates/article-10-96-1327.jsp. (Accessed April 14, 2004).

13 Ibid.

14 Ibid.

15 Ibid.

16 Tariq Ramadan "L'islam d'Europe sort de l'isolement," *Le Monde Diplomatique*, April 1998, p.13. http://www.monde-diplomatique.fr/1998/04/RAMADAN/10246.html (accessed September 10, 2007).

17 Ibid. During a recent encounter (September 2007) in Novi Pazar in Serbia, the Mufti of that predominantly Muslim city expressed similar pride in his European Muslim identity (with an added emphasis of his *indigenous* European-ness) and also argued that European Islam will not be passive. "It will be either an agent of stability or destabilisation in Europe."

18 *Progressive Muslims: On Justice, Gender and Pluralism*, Omid Safi, ed., (Oxford: Openworld, 2003), pp.1-26.

19 Jocelyne Cesari, "Islam in France: The Shaping Of A Religious Minority," in Yvonne Y Haddad, ed., *Muslims in the West, from Sojourners to Citizens* (Oxford: Oxford University Press, 2002), pp.36-51.

20 See for example Khaled Abou El Fadl, "The ugly modern and the modern ugly: reclaiming the beautiful in Islam," in Safi, *Progressive Muslims*, pp.33-77.

21 Ernest Gellner, *Conditions of Liberty, Civil Society and its Rivals* (London: Hamish Hamilton, 1994). A more succinct restatement of Gellner's thesis can be found in Ernest Gellner, "Foreword," in Ahmed and Donnan, eds., *Islam, Globalization and Postmodernity*, pp.xi-xiv.

22 Bassam Tibi, *Islam Between Culture and Politics* (London: Palgrave, 2001).

23 Ramadan "L'islam d'Europe."

24 The conference titled "Fiqh Today: Muslims as Minorities" was organized by a number of groups led by the Association of Muslim Social Scientists (UK) and held on 21-22 February 2004.

25 Mahmud Al-Rashid, "Tariq Ramadan: 'The Most Dangerous Man in Europe,'" *Emel* Magazine, (May-June, 2005), No. 11.
26 Safi, *Progressive Muslims*, pp.15-17.
27 Abdullahi A. An-Na'im, *Towards an Islamic Reformation: Civil Liberties, Human Rights and International Law* (Syracuse, NY: Syracuse University Press, 1990).
28 Cf. Cesari, *When Islam Meets Democracy*, pp.141-148.
29 A term suggested by a leading advocate of this trend, Abdullah S. Schleifer of the American University in Cairo. American-born Schleifer was NBC correspondent in Cairo when he converted to Islam from Judaism in the 1970's.
30 Muhammad Asad, *Islam at the Crossroads* (Gibraltar: Dar Al-Andalus, 1982), pp.7-8.
31 See Haifaa Jawad "Seyyed Hossein Nasr and the Study of Religion in Contemporary Society," *American Journal of Islamic Social Science* (2005), vol. 22, no. 2, pp.49-68.
32 Maryum Jameelah, "Why I embraced Islam," an excerpt from her book *Islam and Modernism*, posted at http://www.islamfortoday.com/maryumjameelah.htm. (Accessed on November 2002, 2005).
33 Seyyed Hossein Nasr, "Reflections on Islam and Modern Life," *Al-Serat*, (n.d., c. 1980), vol. 6, no 1. http://www.al-islam.org/al-serat/reflect-nasr.htm. (Accessed August 21, 2007).
34 Abdal-Hakim Murad, "Muslim loyalty and belonging: some reflections on the psychosocial background," January 2003, http://www.masud.co.uk/ISLAM/ahm/loyalty.htm. (Accessed April 24, 2005). Murad's views are publicized on a website which boasts of being "one of the web's leading and original resources for traditional Islam since 1996."
35 Murad, "Muslim loyalty and belonging."
36 Ibid.
37 Ibid.
38 H.A.R Gibb, *Modern Trends in Islam* (Chicago: Chicago University Press, 1947); Cf. Michael Kerr, *Islamic Reform. The Political and Legal Theories of Muhammad Abduh and Rashid Rida* (Berkeley: University of California Press, 1966).
39 Abdolkarim Soroush, *Reason, Freedom, and Democracy in Islam: Essential Writings of Abdolkarim Soroush*, M. and A. Sadri, eds., (Oxford: Oxford University Press, 2000).
40 Fazlur Rahman, *Revival and Reform in Islam: A Study of Islamic Fundamentalism*, Ebrahim Moosa, ed., (Oxford: Oneworld, 2000), pp.10-17.
41 Cf. Gerholm, "Two Muslim Intellectuals," pp.206-7.

42 Bakar, "The Intellectual Impact of American Muslim Scholars," p.21.
43 Ibid., pp.15-21. See also Ali Hisyam "Fazlur Rahman and Islamic Liberalism (in) Indonesia," *Liberal Islam Network*, at http://islamlib.com/en/page.php?page=article&id=556, 23 December 2003 (accessed May 25, 2005).
44 Ismail Raji al-Faruqi, *Islamization of Knowledge: General Principles and Work Plan* (Herndon, VA: IIIT, 1989).
45 See note 39 above.
46 See Abdelwahab El-Affendi, *Rethinking Islam and Modernity: Essays in Honour of Fathi Osman* (Leicester: The Islamic Foundation, 2001).
47 Nasr Abu Zayd, *Reformation of Islamic Thought: A Critical Historical Analysis* (Amsterdam: Amsterdam University Press, 2006) pp.98-99.
48 An-Na'im, *Towards an Islamic Reformation.*
49 Daniel Pipes "Stealth Islamist: Khaled Abou El Fadl" *Middle East Quarterly* Spring 2004. http://www.danielpipes.org/article/1841 (accessed June 14, 2005).
50 M. A. Muqtedar Khan, "The Priority of Politics: A response to "Islam and the Challenge of Democracy"," *The Boston Review* (April-May, 2003).
51 Azzam Tamimi, "Liberalism, Democracy and Islam: looking for the odd man out," *The Daily Star*, (Saturday, July 24, 2004). (Also on http://www.mpf.org.my/bookreviews/20040820-islamdemocracy.html. (Accessed on November 15, 2005).
52 Khaled Abou El Fadl, *Speaking in God's Name: Islamic Law, Authority and Women* (Oxford: Oneworld Publications, 2001).
53 Khaled Abou El Fadl, "Speaking, Killing and Loving in God's Name," *The Hedgehog Review*, (Spring 2004), Review 6, no.1. http://www.scholarofthehouse.org/skiandloingo.html. (Accessed May 24, 2005).
54 See *Progressive Muslims: On Justice, Gender and Pluralism*, ed. Omid Safi (Oxford: Oneworld, 2003), pp.1-29.
55 Cesari, *When Islam meets Democracy*, pp.169-174. Cf. ed. Katherine Bullock, *Muslim Women Activists in North America: Speaking for Ourselves* (Austin, Texas: University of Texas).
56 Altaf Bhimji *et. al.*, "Text of A Comment on the formation of PMUNA" November 12, 2004, at: http://commentpmuna.blogspot.com/2004/11/text-of-comment-on-formation-of-pmuna.html. (accessed August 20, 2005).
57 See text of Khan's resignation letter and comments on it at: http://almusawwir.org/progressivemuslims/?p=19#comments. (Accessed August 20, 2005).
58 Muqtedar Khan "Is Muslimwakeup.com Undermining the Progressive Muslim Movement?" May 2, 2005, on http://www.ijtihad.org/Muslimwakeup.htm. (Accessed October 14, 2005).

59 Altaf Bhimji, "Sellouts or Saviors: Saving "Progressive" Muslims from Themselves," *Muslims Wake Up!*, October 26, 2003, on http://www.muslimwakeup.com/main/archives/2003/10/sellouts_or_sav .php. (accessed August 22, 2005).

60 Asef Bayat "What is Post-Islamism?" *ISIM Review*, vol. 16, no. 3 (2005), p5.

61 Gerholm, "Two Muslim intellectuals," p.190-1.

62 See Abdelwahab El-Affendi, "The Elusive Reformation," *Journal of Democracy* (April 2003), vol. 14, no. 2, pp.34-39.

63 Abu Musab, "Euro Islam," *Khilafah.com Journal*, 23 April 2003. (Accessed 19 September 2004).

64 Richard N. Ostling, "U.S. scholar Abou El Fadl says this generation's Muslims face a momentous choice," AP State Wire News, November 5, 2005 at: http://24hour.sacbee.com/state_wire/story/13817345p-14658210c.html. (Accessed November 29, 2005).

65 Al-Rashid, "Tariq Ramadan."

66 Muhammad Abu Rumman, "Al-Tajdid al-Islami bayna al-Tahafut wa al-Jumud," *Al-Ghad*, April 1, 2005. http://alghad.dot.jo/index.php?news=15465. (Accessed September 10, 2007).

67 See www.iiit.org.

68 Amina Wadud, "American Muslim Identity: Race and Ethnicity in Progressive Islam," in Omid Safi, ed., *Progressive Muslims*, pp.270-285.

69 I have obtained partial confirmation for this assertion from my friend Dr Ali Paya, a prominent Iranian intellectual who has extensively researched the influence of major Western philosophers such as Popper and Habermas on the Iranian political scene.